Illustrated Guide to
Carving
Tree Bark

Written by Rick Jensen
Photography by Jack A. Williams

**Fox
Chapel Publishing**

1970 Broad Street • East Petersburg, PA 17520
www.FoxChapelPublishing.com

ACKNOWLEDGMENTS

I would like to express my sincere appreciation for the contributions of the following individuals that made this book possible. First and foremost, thanks to my family and especially my wife, Jody, and my daughter, Jaime, for their invaluable assistance with writing, transcribing and editing materials for this book. In addition, I would also like to thank Irene Bertils, whose artwork was a real complement to this project. Thanks also to Larry and Carol Yudis, owners and managers of The Woodcraft Shop, for the use of their shop for the step-by-step photo session. A very special thank you goes to Carole Williams for all of her photographic editing work and to my co-author, Jack A. Williams, for the photography included in this book, as well as his constant support, guidance and encouragement throughout this project. A special thanks goes to Marshal Artime, president of the National Bark Carvers Association, for his support and encouragement. I'd also like to thank Jim Hilty for his scientific contributions on the growth of bark.—Rick Jensen

Publisher	Alan Giagnocavo
Book Editor	Ayleen Stellhorn
Desktop Specialist	Leah Smirlis
Cover Design	Jon Deck

ISBN 1–56523–218–6

Library of Congress Control Number: 2003116442

To learn more about the other great books
from Fox Chapel Publishing, or to find a
retailer near you, call toll-free 1-800-457-9112
or visit us at **www.FoxChapelPublishing.com**.

Printed in China
10 9 8 7 6 5 4 3 2

Contents

About the Authors

Rick Jensen got his first taste of carving growing up along the Missouri River bottoms in North Dakota. His father supplied him with a pocketknife at the age of seven. Whittling on sticks started what would become a lifetime of woodcarving.

Upon moving to northwestern Minnesota, Rick became interested in art, including drawing and sculpting. His first carved project was done in a high school art class in 1965. Today, that piece hangs in his home as a reminder of what sparked his interest.

Taking several years off from his art, Rick served in Vietnam, gained a post-secondary education, and began to raise his family of three daughters. He resumed carving in 1984.

Soon after, Rick became interested in woodcarving shows and competitions. While showing his work, he was often approached with the idea of sharing his talent with others by teaching them to carve. He now travels throughout the Midwest and Canada hosting woodcarving seminars.

Some awards he has received at various woodcarving competitions include Best of Show, People's Choice, Judge's Choice and Best Table Display, in addition to numerous first and second place awards. Rick has judged carving shows in Canada, Montana and Minnesota.

Rick feels very fortunate to have been chosen by his peers to have his work included in the book, *Carving Found Wood* by Vic Hood and Jack A. Williams. Other artistic endeavors of Rick's include antler carving, bone carving and stone carving.

Jack A. Williams is a commercial photographer working from his studio in Knoxville, Tennessee. Photography was once a hobby for Jack until he discovered he could make a living doing what he enjoyed. He then needed a new hobby, so in 1973 he started woodcarving. His first project involved carving an eagle from scrap lumber, not knowing that scrap lumber was not a recommended carving wood.

Undaunted, Jack continued carving. He has since won a third Best of Show in the first National Caricature Carving Competition, a Best of Show at the Ward Wildfowl Carving competition, the People's and Carver's Choice and Best of Wood Sculpture at Dollywood and a Best of Division at the International Woodcarvers Congress. Jack also won first place in the Flex-Cut Tool Internet Carving Competition in 2001.

In addition to carving, Jack is also active in the carving community. October 2003 marked the twelfth year for him to coordinate the woodcarving show at Dollywood and the first year to coordinate the National Caricature Carving Competition and Exhibit, also held at Dollywood. He is also a founding member and the current president of the Tennessee Carvers Guild. Jack's artistic talents have been acknowledged by his peers with an invitation in 2003 to join the Caricature Carvers of America.

Jack now spends a great deal of time photographing carvings at shows and for friends, and his photography appears frequently in many magazines on woodcarving and other subjects. Along with Vic Hood, Jack co-authored *Carving Found Wood* and *Extreme Pumpkin Carving*, both published by Fox Chapel Publishing Company.

Why I Carve Bark

Cottonwood bark is my choice as the ultimate media for carving due to its rough exterior surface and the beautiful red and gold tones found in the interior of the bark. On average, cottonwood bark is one of the easiest carving materials to use due to its softness, but I have found an occasional piece to be nearly as hard as rock. These, thankfully, are few and far between.

When I began carving bark, I followed the trend and carved wood spirits like so many other carvers. I found this to be fun but looked to find a more individual way of challenging my progressing carving skills. I soon found that more unique shapes better held my interest. Over time, I learned to take advantage of the natural irregularities and textures in cottonwood bark, using them to create carvings of whimsical houses and castles.

Back then I thought the best kind of bark for carving was five inches thick, five inches wide and two feet long. These approximate dimensions were wonderful for realistic face carving and for wood spirits. My ideas concerning the "perfect" piece of bark have most certainly changed.

I now purposely look for twisted, gnarled, uniquely shaped pieces of cottonwood bark. Some of the bark I pick up almost tells me what to carve just by its basic shape. With these pieces, I can create lighthouses, churches, tree houses and more. I utilize natural flaws and lines in the bark to enhance my whimsical creations.

I believe that you can force any carving out of a block of basswood or butternut, but when carving a whimsical house or other figure in bark, the bark truly leads you in the right direction. For this very reason, my houses are like fingerprints. There will never be two that are exactly alike.

Shanty on Beaver Creek
1½" thick, 3" wide, 8" long
Carved from Eastern Cottonwood Bark;
lacquer and wax finish

Breezeway
4" thick, 4" wide, 16" long
Carved from Black Cottonwood Bark;
shoe cream finish

The Penthouse
3½ " thick, 4" wide, 11" long
Carved from Plains Cottonwood Bark;
lacquer and wax finish

On Shakey Ground
4" thick, 5" wide, 10" long
Carved from Plains Cottonwood Bark;
lacquer and wax finish

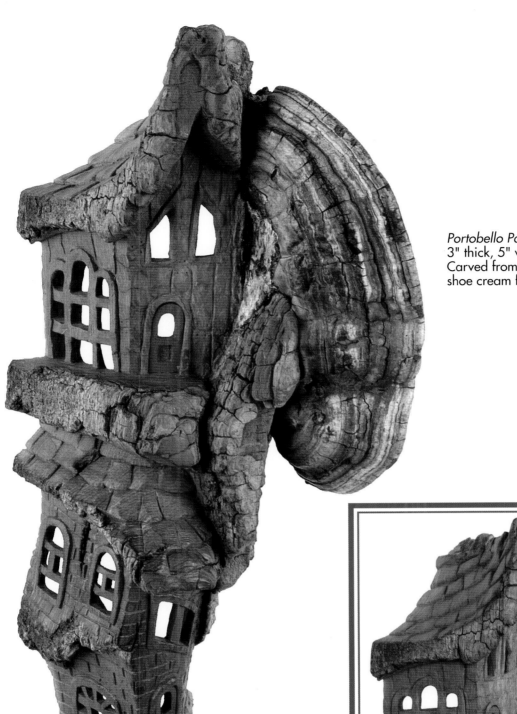

Portobello Palace
3" thick, 5" wide, 15" long
Carved from Eastern Cottonwood Bark;
shoe cream finish

Untitled Santa
2½" thick, 3¾" wide, 8" long
Carved from Eastern Cottonwood Bark;
acrylic paint, lacquer and wax finish

Untitled Santa
2½" thick, 3½" wide, 11½" long
Carved from Eastern Cottonwood Bark;
acrylic paint, lacquer and wax finish

GALLERY

North Shore Breeze
3" thick, 4" wide, 16" long
Carved from Plains Cottonwood Bark;
lacquer and wax finish

On-A-Slant Villa
3" thick, 3" wide, 16" long
Carved from Plains Cottonwood Bark;
lacquer and wax finish

GALLERY

Chateau Par La Mer
5" thick, 6" wide, 23" long
Carved from Plains Cottonwood Bark;
lacquer and wax finish

Island Retreat
2½" thick, 4" wide, 16" long
Carved from Plains Cottonwood Bark;
briwax finish

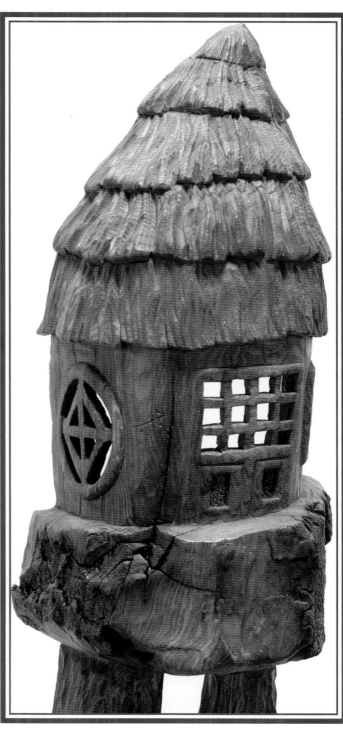

North Shore Retreat
4" thick, 5" wide, 17" long
Carved from Black Cottonwood Bark;
lacquer and wax finish

Cottonwood Condo
4" thick, 4¹/₂" wide, 18" long
Carved from Plains Cottonwood Bark;
lacquer and wax finish

La Casa Bonita
2" thick, 4" wide, 11" long
Carved from Eastern Cottonwood Bark;
lacquer and wax finish

Untitled Santa
1½" thick, 3" wide, 6" long
Carved from Eastern Cottonwood Bark;
acrylic paint, lacquer and wax finish

Untitled Santa
3" thick, 4" wide,
16" long
Carved from Plains
Cottonwood Bark; acrylic
paint, lacquer and wax finish

Untitled Wood Spirit
4½" thick, 4¾" wide, 20" long
Carved from Black Cottonwood Bark;
lacquer finish no wax

Untitled Wood Spirit
4" thick, 6" wide, 23" long
Carved from Plains Cottonwood Bark
(also called Minnesota Red);
lacquer and wax finish

GALLERY

Untitled Wood Spirit
3" thick, 5" wide, 17" long
Carved from Plains Cottonwood Bark;
shoe cream finish

Untitled Wood Spirit
4" thick, 4" wide, 16" long
Carved from Black Cottonwood Bark
(Montana Gold);
shoe cream finish

About Cottonwood Bark

Dead layers of the cottonwood tree's food-conducting layers are not sloughed off. Instead they are compressed and build upon each other until they comprise many layers, each only a few thousandths of an inch thick. These layers form the grain of the bark. This piece of bark is 162 years old.

 ccording to Jim Hilty, Professor Emeritus at the University of Tennessee, who holds a Ph.D. in Botany and Plant Pathology, in addition to being an award-winning carver, "The word 'bark' has various meanings but is most commonly used as a non-technical term referring to the tough exterior covering of woody stems and roots. Bark is composed, in part, of dead food-conducting tissue that is displaced outward by the annual production of new food-conducting layers by the trees' formative tissue, the cambium. In western cottonwood these dead layers are not sloughed off but are compressed and accumulate into a thick bark covering that is suitable for carving."

When cutting a cross section of a piece of bark, one can easily notice that the bark is made up of many layers that measure only a few thousandths of an inch thick. These layers form the grain of the bark, which can create unique swirl patterns within the piece. Each layer of bark represents one year of growth.

COTTONWOODS OF NORTH AMERICA

Seven species of cottonwood grow on the North American continent: Eastern cottonwood, Plains cottonwood, black cottonwood, swamp cottonwood, Freemont cottonwood, Palmer cottonwood and narrow leaf cottonwood.

Eastern cottonwood, sometimes referred to as Southern cottonwood, swamp wood, Carolina poplar, Eastern poplar or necklace poplar, grows along the stream and river bottom lands of Quebec, Canada, westward into North Dakota, southwest to Manitoba, south to central Texas and east to northwestern Florida and Georgia. The western boundary is not well defined due to the overlapping ranges of the Eastern cottonwood and the Plains cottonwood ranges.

Figure 1:
Eastern cottonwood

Figure 2:
Plains cottonwood

Figure 3:
Black cottonwood

Eastern cottonwood is one of the tallest tree species east of the Rocky Mountains with heights up to 190 feet and diameters up to six feet. Eastern cottonwood hybridizes with Plains cottonwood and crosses with several other tree species. It is believed that these crosses are what cause thicker and wider bark on trees in areas where this variety of tree is not commonly found. **(See Figure 1.)**

I have carved many pieces of Eastern cottonwood bark and find it easy to carve.

Plains cottonwood is also known as Texas cottonwood, river cottonwood, Western cottonwood and Plains poplar. It grows from southern Alberta, central Saskatchewan and southwestern Manitoba, Canada, south throughout the Great Plains into North Dakota, South Dakota, Nebraska, Wyoming, Colorado, Montana, Kansas and western Oklahoma. It continues to spread into north central Texas and extreme northeastern New Mexico.

The bark from Plains cottonwood trees is usually wider and thicker than that of the Eastern cottonwood, thus making it more desirable for carving. **(See Figure 2.)** This type of bark is used in the step-by-step demonstration of carving a whimsical house.

Black cottonwood has a growth range that extends from western Wyoming to include western Montana, Idaho, northern Utah, Nevada, northern California, Oregon, Washington, British Columbia, the Yukon and the coast of Alaska.

Black cottonwood bark is a silvery gray color that turns black when wet. It is the thickest and widest cottonwood bark to grow in North America. It tends to be between three and six inches thick and up to six inches wide. Black cottonwood bark is ideal for carving. **(See Figure 3.)**

Black cottonwood produces the best bark for carving. The bark of the black cottonwood tree is the widest and thickest of all the cottonwood species and carves especially well.

Swamp cottonwood grows along the southern Mississippi Valley and along the coastlines of Louisiana, Mississippi and Alabama, and into the panhandle of Florida. It is also found along the coastlines of Georgia, North Carolina, South Carolina and Virginia.

Swamp cottonwood can grow to heights nearing 90 feet with a three- to four-foot trunk diameter. The bark of older trees is an auburn color and has a slightly shaggy appearance.

I have not personally carved swamp cottonwood bark.

Freemont cottonwood grows along the Gulf of California in Mexico, the eastern edge of Arizona and the western edge of New Mexico near Albuquerque.

Freemont cottonwood grows to nearly 60 feet tall and has a trunk diameter of three to four feet. On older trees, the thick, deeply furrowed bark is a dark reddish-brown color. **(See Figure 4.)**

I find Freemont cottonwood bark somewhat more difficult to carve than the previously mentioned species. It is more porous than Eastern cottonwood bark and black cottonwood bark, but with care, it can be carved.

Palmer cottonwood grows in a relatively small area along the Mexico and Texas border. It reaches heights of sixty feet with a three to four foot trunk diameter. The bark of a mature tree is a gray-brown color and is deeply furrowed, somewhat resembling the bark of Eastern cottonwood.

I have not carved Palmer cottonwood bark, but because of its physical similarities to Eastern cottonwood, I believe that its carving properties would be similar as well.

Narrow leaf cottonwood is found in Mexico, Arizona, New Mexico, Utah, Colorado, Wyoming, Idaho and Montana, and in parts of southern British Columbia and Alberta, Canada. It grows to about 60 feet in height with a trunk diameter of one and a half to two feet. The bark is dark brown with deep furrows on mature trees.

Narrow leaf cottonwood bark is hard to identify. I have not carved any of this type of bark, but I have heard from other carvers that it can be carved.

FINDING COTTONWOOD BARK

I find my supplies of cottonwood bark in a variety of places. Most

Figure 4:
Freemont cottonwood

commonly, I search the river bottoms near the flood plains in Minnesota, along the Missouri River in North Dakota and in the areas following the Yellowstone River and the Clark Fork River in Montana.

I have been fortunate to discover black cottonwood nearly eight inches thick along the Red Lake River near my home in northwestern Minnesota. I have also found similar bark along the Red River of the North, which flows north into Lake Winnipeg, Manitoba, Canada.

My recommendations for finding bark, beyond searching along river bottoms, include looking along creeks and coulees and on old homesteads.

COLOR VARIATIONS OF BARK

Upon removing the rough outer layer of bark, the interior colors may vary from a golden color to a reddish-gold hue. These variations are a direct result of minerals in the soil where the tree grew.

The bark that I collect locally in northwestern Minnesota carries a reddish color. Bark pieces from North Dakota and Montana carry a more golden tone. Many carvers refer to the bark as Minnesota Red, Dakota Red and Montana Gold.

Do not remove cottonwood bark from live trees. Bark is especially hard to remove from live trees, and it will break into pieces of unusable size if you attempt to cut it from the tree. Only bark from dead or dying trees—bark that can be pulled from the trunk of a tree with your hands—should be harvested for bark carving purposes.

HARVESTING BARK

When harvesting cottonwood bark, I tend to look for old, dying or dead trees, such as those that have been hit by lightning or blown over in a windstorm. It can take two to three years once a tree has started to die for the bark to begin to loosen and fall off. This is the bark that is most desirable for woodcarving.

All of the bark that I use can be removed from dead or dying trees with my bare hands. No special tools are needed. It is nearly impossible to remove bark suitable for carving from a live tree. Attempting to do so will only result in small chunks of bark chipping off and great harm to the tree.

CLEANING AND STORING BARK

When I gather bark from river bottoms, it has often been exposed to flood waters and contains much dirt, silt and other sediments. To remove a majority of these unwanted deposits, I wash the bark using a spray nozzle attachment on a garden hose and a scrub brush. No matter where cottonwood bark is located or how well it is cleaned, it will always contain a bit of dirt and have some grit to it; however, the end results far outweigh the small inconvenience provided by unwanted materials.

I store my bark outdoors due to the insects—spiders, worms and larvae—that tend to live in the bark. At times, I place the bark that I plan to utilize in a plastic bag and use a fumigant to rid it of inhabitants. It is important to follow all of the manufacturer's directions when using a fumigant.

When storing cottonwood bark outdoors, elevate it a few inches above the ground, loosely crisscrossing the pieces in order to keep moisture from drawing into the bark. If extended storage is necessary, consider building a roof over the top of the bark pile, but don't allow the space to become airtight. If bark is stored in an airtight area, it will become punky and rotten in the center, rendering it unusable.

Bark Carving Basics

Due to the grain structure of the bark, some difficulties may arise during carving. With a little knowledge and some foresight, most of these problems can be dealt with as you are carving, thereby avoiding disastrous results that may render your carving unsalvageable.

CUTTING CROSS-GRAIN

For example, when carving a face, the grain may interfere with small detail work, like eyebrows. In order to create fine, defining hairs, a 2 mm #11 gouge may be used. Starting at the beginning point of the eyebrow (that closest to the nose), you will have the first few cuts go well because they are parallel to the grain. The next cuts will start parallel to the grain and make a sharp turn, lying down as they go toward the outside of the face. Because the carving goes from running parallel to the grain to across the grain, this area is where bark tends to flake, crumble or tear. To avoid this hazard, use a 6 mm #11 gouge and lightly break up the eyebrow mass. This process creates a wider cut through the cross-grain, lessening the chance for damage to the bark.

An alternate way to remedy a tear is to use power tools. Contrary to some beliefs, bark carves extremely well with power. Chuck up either a ball-shaped diamond or a coarse ruby ball. Or, for a dynamic effect, utilize three differently sized, ball-shaped cutters, starting with the largest and progressing down to the smallest. Using the cutters, carve in the detail, such as hair, right through the cross-grain. Utilizing power across the cross-grain does not stress the wood and eliminates some of the tear-out.

Silent Sentinel
3½" thick, 6" wide, 22" long
Carved from Plains Cottonwood Bark;
lacquer and wax finish

CARVING SOFT AREAS

Bark is very soft. This softness creates some problems with knife and chisel work; therefore, I recommend a compound cutting action.

Imagine slicing a loaf of bread with a non-serrated kitchen knife. The loaf would crush. If a compound action of pushing and pulling is combined with the downward force, it will slice clean. This same principle is applied when using a knife on bark.

Any time a soft wood, such as cottonwood bark, is cut, it is important to keep the tool edges extremely sharp. If the edges aren't sharp, the fiber will shear and mash, rather than cut. Always keep tools sharp!

EASING STRESS

Another technique employed to ensure clean cuts is called "sneaking up on a cut." To use this technique, make a stop cut ahead of where the actual cut is going to end up. Then remove the wood up to the temporary stop cut. Repeat this process until the final destination is reached. Following this technique also helps to reduce stress on the bark, again eliminating some of the tear-out and flake-off. (A demonstration of this technique is shown in Chapter Three.)

TOOLS FOR BARK CARVING

The following is a list of tools that I commonly use in carving bark. Because my specialty is carving whimsical houses in bark, I have described the uses of these tools as they apply to carving those houses. If you decide to carve wood spirits or Santas or other figures, you will find that some of these tools have comparable uses for detailing facial features or carving hair.

If you decide to work with hand tools, keep in mind that carving with hand tools takes longer than carving with power tools. Hand tools also tend to generate more stress on the wood than power tools. Make sure that the bark you choose to carve with hand tools is thick enough to support your cuts and the pressure.

The tools listed below are suggestions. Tools of your choice may be used to accomplish the same uses.

HAND TOOLS

TOOL	USE
#4 or #5 20 mm gouge	Use for rough-in work
$\frac{1}{2}$" - 12 mm v-tool	Use for rough-in and roof work
$\frac{1}{4}$" - 6 mm v-tool	Use around trim work
$\frac{3}{32}$" - 2.5 mm v-tool	Use in making brick work
$\frac{1}{2}$" - #3 fishtail gouge	Use for cleanup
$\frac{1}{4}$" - #3 long bent fishtail gouge	Use in cleanup around window trim
$\frac{3}{16}$" - #3 long bent gouge	Use in cleanup around window trim
#5 16 mm bent palm gouge	Use in removing the back of the carving
Knife – short blade	Use for detail work
Knife – long blade	Use for rough-in work and stop cuts
4 or 6 mm #11 gouge	Use in texturing cottonwood bark trees

ROTARY TOOLS

TOOL	USE
NSK Micromotor Tool	Use for most power carving
Low torque rotary tool	Use for scuffing the carving
Foredom Flex Shaft Machine	Use with a horsehair brush to buff the carving after it has been waxed

BURS

2.3 mm cylinder stump cutter	Use to open up windows and doors
$^{3}/_{32}$" shank coarse ruby (flame shape)	Use in carving rocks
$^{3}/_{32}$" shank needle point diamond	Use in carving rocks
$^{1}/_{8}$" shank blue typhoon ball	Use in removing the back of the carving
$^{1}/_{8}$" shank blue typhoon dovetail	Use in removing the back of the carving

POWER TOOLS

WOODBURNER: A woodburner with a skew tip is used to create stop cuts around windows and doors. (A small v-tool can also be used).

DUST COLLECTOR: This is a must if you power carve. You may also want to wear a dust mask.

GLUES

YELLOW CARPENTER'S WOOD GLUE, along with bark dust, can be used to repair mistakes. This is the method that I used in the following step-by-step.

CYANOACRYLATE GLUE, otherwise known as CA glue or Super Glue™, is used to fill cracks and splits. I use super thin CA glue, along with accelerator, to set the glue instantly. When using CA glues, it's a good idea to always have some de-bonder on hand in case of a mishap. Be sure to read and follow all label directions.

Mix a small amount of bark dust with Yellow Carpenter's Wood Glue to make repairs.

SHARPENING

Over the years, I have come to realize that many carvers greatly dislike sharpening tools. Nevertheless, it is my experience that sharp tools are essential to good carving. Sharp tools make the carving process easier as well as improve upon the quality of work.

A majority of carving tools and knives arrive from the factory without a sharp edge. They must be sharpened and honed before use. I have often thought about first-time carvers giving up in utter frustration, believing they don't have the talent to be a woodcarver, when it is really a dull tool that is the problem. Carving with sharp tools is a joy that must be experienced to be appreciated.

Much has been written in both magazines and books detailing the art of sharpening. *Wood Carving Illustrated*, published by Fox Chapel Publishing Company, has several well-written, informative articles on tool sharpening, as does the National Woodcarver's Association magazine, *Chip Chats*. Internationally recognized woodcarver and author, Harold Enlow, provides detailed information on the sharpening and honing of knives, chisels, gouges and v-tools in his books. These publications and others, along with videos, may be purchased through a carving supplier.

Carving clubs are another excellent source of sharpening help. Most clubs have a few carvers who are quite proficient at sharpening tools. Ask one of these carvers for help in sharpening, or set aside a club night for hands-on sharpening demonstrations.

I, personally, learned to sharpen all of my tools using stones and various pieces of leather. About fifteen years ago, I converted to power sharpening. I currently use various dry grinding systems, water wheels and high speed buffing units for my sharpening needs. I am able to sharpen a tool in five minutes, whereas it used to take me about an hour to sharpen the same tool. Whichever method of sharpening you choose, stay with it. Become proficient at sharpening, and your tools will have the ultimate edge.

This photo depicts the 3M Scotch-Brite 7440 pads and rotary tool, which are utilized for the scuffing process that takes the place of sanding. The Scotch-Brite pads are available in a rectangular-shaped sheet. Because I prefer using circular-shaped pads, I create my own. These are made by punching out the circular shape with a 1½"-diameter thin wall pipe that has been sharpened on one end and a hammer. When scuffing, I use a single pad with a low-torque rotary tool. Because the bark is quite soft, remember to utilize a light touch.

MISCELLANEOUS TOOLS

TOOL	USE
¼" drill bit	Use to create a hole for hanging the carving
³/₃₂" drill bit	Use in drilling windows and doors
Needle files	Use to shape and clean out window and door openings
Double ball end stylus	Use to make nail holes and vertical siding
Short scratch awl	Use to develop texture on doors, etc.
Stiff bristle brush	Use for cleaning the carving
Shoe brush	Use for buffing the carving
Horsehair rotary brush	Use for buffing the carving
7440 Scotch-Brite pad	Use for cleaning and softening the hard lines left from carving
³/₃₂" shank screw head mandrill	Use with Scotch-Brite pad
Small brass brush on a mandrill	Use with rotary tool to remove dried glue

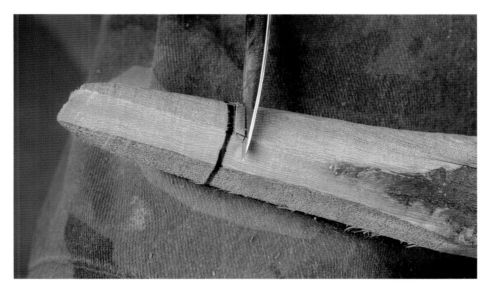

SPECIAL CUTS

Before you begin the step-by-step demonstration, take a close look at the special cuts and repair techniques featured in this chapter.

THE COMPOUND CUT

A knife is being used to make a stop cut in a piece of bark in preparation for the next step.

This photo illustrates the use of a compound cut. Note the location of the knife tip. Using downward force and a forward-pushing motion at the same time, begin the cut.

Continue with the downward force and forward-pushing motion. Notice that the knife is being slid from the tip to the heel as the cut is being made. This action helps create a clean cut and lessens the stress on the bark, creating less tear-out.

SNEAKING UP ON A CUT

A line has been drawn on the bark to establish a final stop cut location. Create a temporary stop cut in front of the final cut, and remove the bark up to the temporary stop cut line.

A knife is being used in this photo to make a thin, downward cut on the final stop cut line to clean up the cut.

The end result is illustrated in this photo showing the clean, final stop cut that has been obtained by "sneaking up" on the final stop cut line.

REPAIR

A different carving is being utilized in this photo to demonstrate how to fix a blowout, or hole, created in the carving when hollowing out the back where the wall and the roofline meet. This is a common mistake that's easily repaired.

Ground-up bark dust, along with yellow carpenter's glue, can be used to make a filler. Mix the dust and the glue together to form a stiff, putty-like consistency.

Begin by applying the putty mixture into the blowout from the backside of the carving so that some of the putty exudes to the front. Allow the putty to dry before continuing. When the putty has dried, carve off the excess putty on the front side of the carving, and smooth and blend in the excess on the back.

The finished repair is illustrated in this photo. The color of the repair will always be a bit darker than the original color of the bark.

This is an example of another type of blowout that can occur. This blowout is more difficult to remedy than the previously illustrated one because the putty mixture does not work as well in this situation.

In this situation, proceed by wetting down the area around the blowout with water, and then use a torch to burn and char the hole, being careful not to overdo it. Caution: Torches must be used outside. See Step 110 on page 51 and the manufacturer's usage instructions for additional safety considerations.)

This photo shows the results of this type of repair. It looks as though the woodland spirits were quick to put out the fire before any major damage could be done.

Carving a Whimsical House

La Maison De Livre
4" thick, 4½" wide, 16" long
Carved from Plains Cottonwood Bark;
lacquer and wax finish

When carving whimsical houses, fantasy castles, lighthouses, churches and cottonwood condos, I rely heavily on my own imagination. Along with my ideas, I do use a variety of reference material.

Much of my reference material is in the form of books, coloring books, calendars and photographs. Another place to gather information on houses, doors and windows comes from observing buildings in my own community. Paying attention to rooflines is beneficial in noticing how they tie into one another, forming valleys and pitches. I also recommend a visit to your local building center. They have many brochures available that show unique styles on windows and doors, such as round tops and arches. You may also wish to search the Internet for additional structural ideas. It is my suggestion to begin a file of collected reference material, and soon you will be on your way to creating wonderful, whimsical bark carvings.

A piece of Plains cottonwood bark, which is approximately 16" long, 4" thick and 4¹⁄₂" wide at its widest point, is used for this project. This bark comes from a large storm-damaged tree near my home in Northwest Minnesota.

As is often the case, I didn't know what I was going to carve until I had this piece of bark in my hands just before the photo shoot. I knew, in the back of my mind, the techniques that I wanted to explain in this demonstration but had no solid idea of how to present them. As I turned the piece over in my hands several times, noting the flaws in the natural bark, an image started to form. I often refer to this type of inspiration as "the bark talking to me." The result is the bark house that you will see carved here.

Note: It is recommended that the complete step-by-step process be reviewed before beginning your project. This will provide a better understanding of what the end result will look like and aid in laying out your initial design.

CREATING A PHOTO REFERENCE LIBRARY

Gathering reference material doesn't have to be costly or a burden. Photographs like these pictures of stone walls can be taken anywhere at anytime. Or keep a sketchbook handy to record odd-shaped windows, such as the ones on the previous pages. When you're ready to carve, pull out this reference material for inspiration and detail.

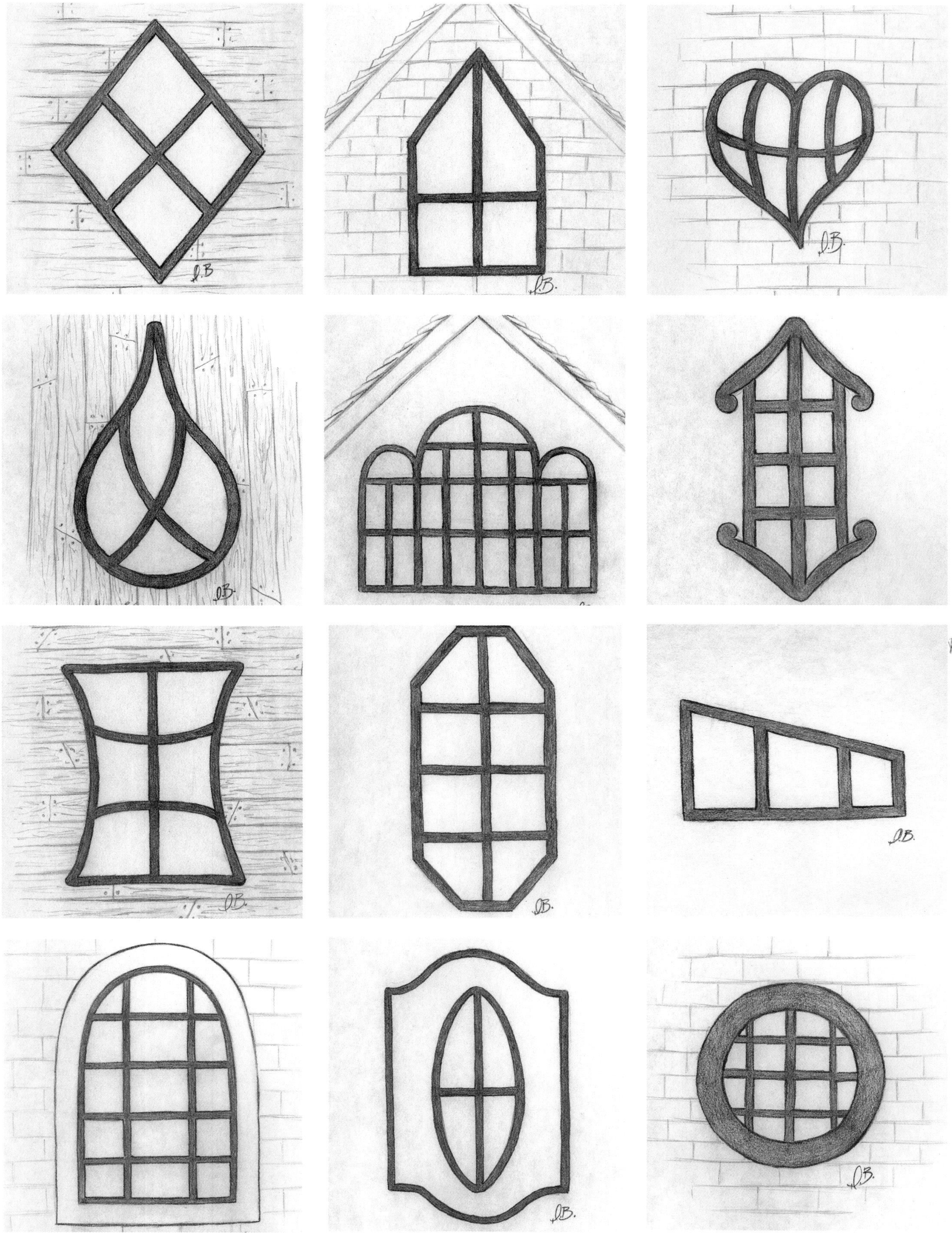

Looking at the top left corner, you will see what looks like a natural roofline with the tallest point becoming a roof peak. The large piece of bark that curves to the left will become the center of the little house, along with some steps and rocks leading to the front door.

Step 1

This is the right side of the bark that will be carved. Note the top right corner. This natural shape will become part of the chimney. Also, note the natural split midway down on the piece of bark on the far right side. This will be saved for future development.

Step 2

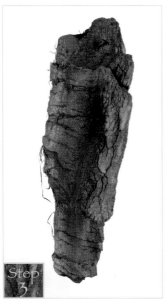

This is the left side of the piece of bark. Notice the hole a few inches from the top. This will become the eave or roofline.

Step 3

Step 4

The bottom black line will be used as the eave and roofline.

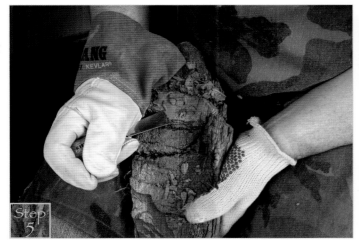

Step 5

Using a #5 1" gouge, begin to shape the left side of the roof. I am wearing a cut-proof Kevlar glove and a leather glove to protect my hands as I carve.

Step 6

Notice the hollowed-out shape that is being created using the #5 gouge for roughing out. Remember to think in terms of flowing or curved lines and to stay away from straight, hard lines.

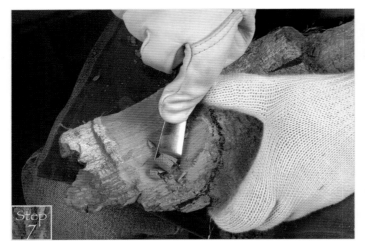

Still using the #5 1" gouge, remove the bark from the right side roof, maintaining the hollowed-out, curved look.

Using a marker or pencil, establish the bottom of the roofline on the front of the carving. This will form the peak of the roof.

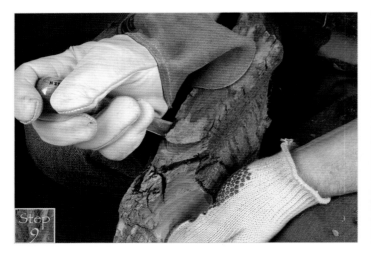

Begin to remove the bark below the roofline using the same #5 gouge. This will allow the roof to protrude past the house.

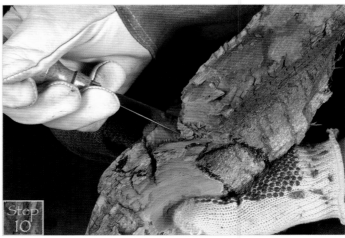

In this photo, the eave is being set in along the roofline with the #5 gouge. You may prefer to use a v-tool for this step. Once a stop cut has been established along the eave, relieve a little of the wood from below it.

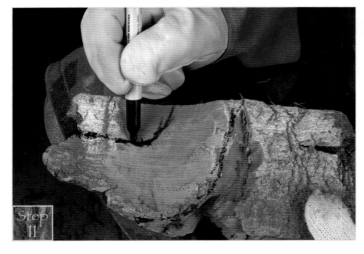

Draw in the chimney with a pencil, maintaining a gentle curve toward the bottom. In this photo, you are able to see the curve of the roof, along with the set-in of the eave.

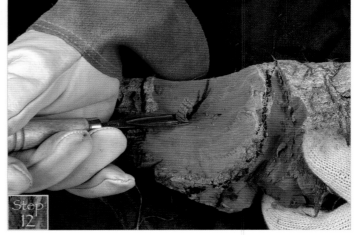

Using a ½" 12 mm v-tool, cut along the line to set in the chimney. Once a stop cut has been created, relieve some of the roof to make the chimney stand out, remembering to continue with the curved flow of the roofline.

Using the #5 gouge, clean off some of the rough bark on the chimney. This will create a place for some brickwork later on. Note that some of the rough bark has been left at the top of the chimney. This rough exterior will enhance the look of the carving.

Continue carving the roof to the peak where the rooflines will join together to form the ridge of the roof.

Roughing out the right side of the roof is now complete. Notice how the rough bark is left along the eave on the front of the roof. This rough bark should be saved for now.

Returning to the left side of the carving, continue to shape the roof, remembering to maintain the hollowed-out, curved appearance.

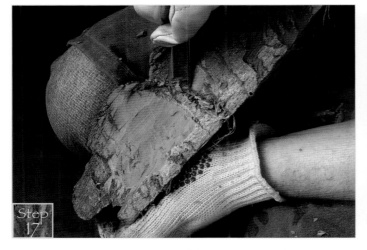

When the stop cut at the bottom of the eaves is complete, relieve the wood from below to make the eaves stand out.

Roughing out the left side of the roof is now complete. Again, notice how the rough bark has been left on the eave and the front of the roof along the top.

CHAPTER 3

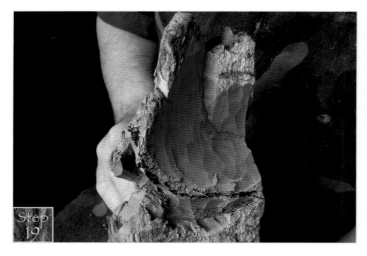

This photo shows the progress thus far. It also shows how far the roof goes in to make the chimney stand out. Notice that the lower, left roof overhang is now starting to show.

Using a large #5 gouge, start to set back the front of the house. Don't take a lot off at this time. Remove just enough to clean off the front.

Continue to clean off the front of the house using the #5 rough-out gouge. Note that I haven't gone very far down on the carving. This process is used to create a taper toward the roofline, while leaving the bottom of the house thick.

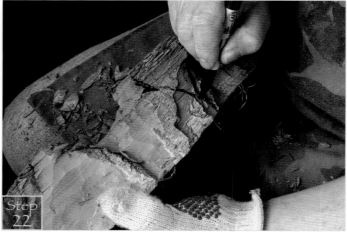

With a marker, draw a line straight across the front of the carving, dropping towards the left side. Using a ½" 12mm v-tool, make a stop cut along this line. This cut will become the top of the foundation.

Using the #5 gouge, relieve the wood down to the foundation line. Repeat this process until the foundation line is approximately ½" deep.

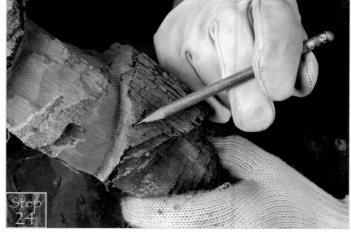

The pencil in this photo is pointing to the top of the foundation line, which continues straight across the front of the carving. Relieving just enough wood to get a foundation line for the stairs creates a bulge in the left wall of the house. Some of the rough bark was left on this bulge area to create a more whimsical look.

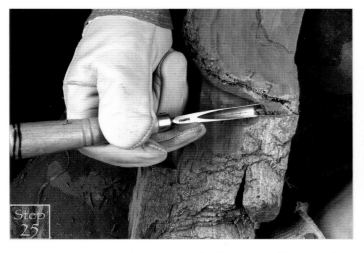

Step 25

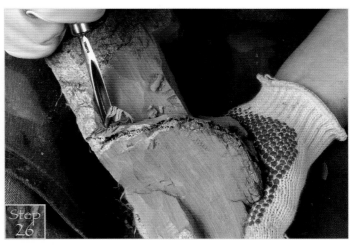

Step 26

In Step 2, it was noted that the natural split area would be saved for future development. It is now time to begin work on this area. Using the ½" 12 mm v-tool, begin by cleaning up under the eave of the roof.

Using the same v-tool as in the previous step, begin to make a column of brick, leaving it wider at the bottom and narrower toward the top.

Step 27

Step 28

In this photo, the v-tool is being used to create a stop cut that joins the brick column and the existing foundation.

This photo shows a profile of the front of the house. Note the landing and the front wall. Also, notice the brick column developing nicely.

Step 29

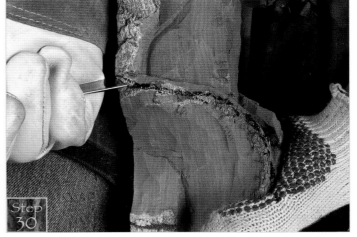

Step 30

Using the #5 gouge, relieve some of the wood up to the split in the bark. Caution: Do not remove more bark than necessary at this point.

Using the #5 gouge, create a shallow stop cut where the roofline and the rock column meet.

Using a #5 gouge, relieve the upper portion of the brick column so that it lies underneath the roofline.

Using a scuffing pad, remove the black marker or pencil lines from the carving, being careful not to remove the rough exterior bark. Note that some of the marked areas are cracked and loose and may require a small amount of glue to hold them together.

Apply a small amount of CA glue to the cracks and splits in the top rough section, being cautious not to spill excess glue on the carving.

Note that the CA glue has soaked into some of the cracks. At this point, a little more glue may be added to the cracks and splits.

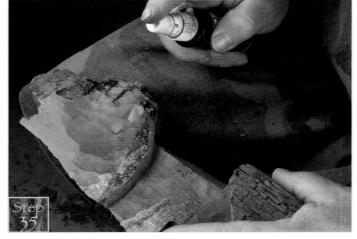

At this point, use an accelerator to set the CA glue instantly. (Use extreme caution when doing this since it forms a chemical reaction that generates a high amount of heat to the point that smoke may be seen rising from the bark.)

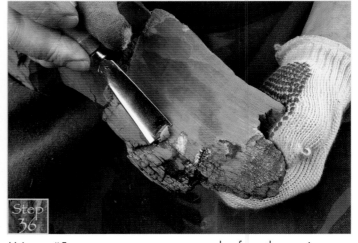

Using a #5 gouge, remove any excess glue from the carving.

Begin drawing in the lines that will become shingles. Note that the lines have some curve to them and that they are not equally spaced. Continue on with the left side of the roof as well.

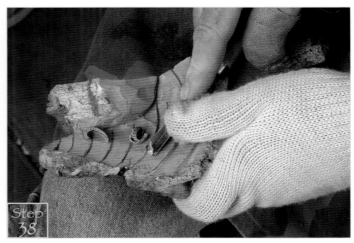

A ½" v-tool is used to begin cutting the rows of shingles. Note how the tool is being used on its side to create a stepped look. Remember when cutting in these lines that the bottom shingle goes under the top shingle. Also, cut in the left side of the roof at this time.

The #5 gouge is used to taper the bottom row of shingles under the top row in this photo.

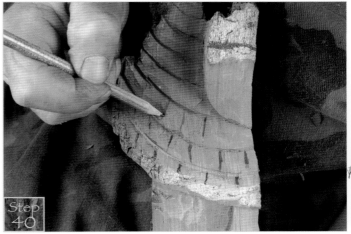

Using a pencil or a marker, draw in each individual shingle, making some shingles wider than others and, above all, avoiding a set pattern. Try not to have all the lines for the shingles straight; a little offset will really enhance the project. Repeat the process on the left side of the roof.

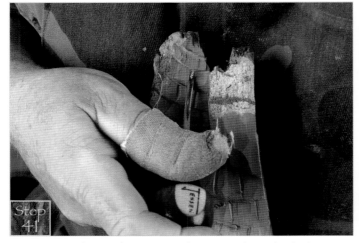

A 4 mm v-tool is used to cut in and separate the individual shingles at this time.

After separating the shingles with a v-tool, a knife is used to create a stop cut in each shingle separation.

Using a knife, take a thin cut off one side of each shingle so that it tapers into the shingle adjoining it. Strong shadow lines, which will add further definition to the shingles, will be created by this cut.

This picture shows the results of Step 43. Note the ½" #3 gouge being using to taper the shingles to the side.

A #3 gouge is being used in this step, in place of a knife, to taper the shingles to the side.

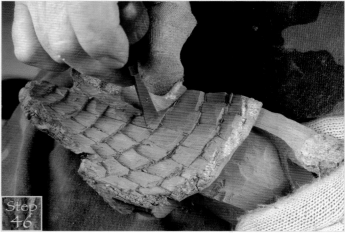

Note the different lengths in the rows of shingles that have been created using a #3 gouge. By creating shingles of varying lengths, a hard, stiff look can be avoided, resulting in a much more pleasing appearance.

A detail knife is being used to cut out a wedge-shaped piece in a shingle, creating a more natural look.

When laying out doors and windows on the carving, be aware of the following three things: 1) Make sure to have a tool that can be used for cleaning around the framework. I prefer a ³⁄₁₆" or ¼" long bent #3 gouge for clean-up work. 2) Make sure the window and door openings are set in from the edge of the building. 3) Draw the windows and the doors wide, similar to the example in this photo.

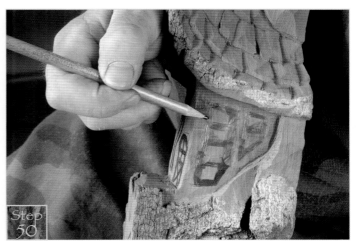

Continue laying out the doors and the windows, noting the width of the frames. Shade in the frames for a clearer picture of how they will look when completed.

Note the distance the window is set back from the front wall. Also note the clearance space left around the windows. This clearance and setback are very important.

Using a wood burner with a skew-type tip, begin burning in the stop cuts. Burn the inside of the windows first, being careful not to burn the stop cuts through the framework. A small v-tool could also be used to create the stop cuts in this step.

Continue on by burning the stop cuts on the outer framework. Again, note the wide framework.

This is a view of the front of the carving showing a round top, crossbuck-style door. Note the setback of the door and the windows from the side walls.

Continue by burning in the rest of the stop cuts.

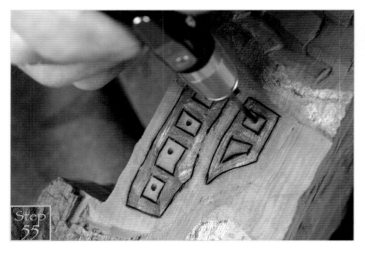

An NSK Micromotor tool with a ³⁄₃₂" drill bit is being used in this photo to drill out the windows. The drilling of the windows, at this point, will provide a location guide when the back of the carving is removed.

A 2.3 mm cylinder stump cutter in the NSK is used to remove the bark inside the window frames. For handcarving, use a small #3 gouge to remove the bark inside the window frames.

The cutting end of the stump cutter is approximately ¼" in length. The ¼" length is used as a guide to set the depth of the windows.

With the tip of a knife, deepen the burned-in stop cut to a depth of about ³⁄₃₂". Note the drilled-in holes in the window and the depth of about ¼".

With a ¹⁄₂" #3 gouge, begin removing bark from the walls of the house toward the window. This will allow the window frames to stand out.

A knife is being used to create a stop cut along the roof eave in preparation for removal of the bark between the window and the roof. This photo also shows how much of the wall was removed to allow the window frame to stand out.

Remove bark with a #3 gouge to the stop cut made in the previous step.

A ¼" long bent #3 fishtail gouge is being used to clean up the tight area around the window frame.

The burnt stop cut lines have now all been carefully carved off for a clean look. Following completion of the windows and the door on the front, work will begin on the back of the carving.

Establish a centerline on the back of the carving in preparation for hollowing out the piece. The area with the red marking will become a support or bridge that will be left in place. Without this support bridge, the carving could collapse when hollowed out.

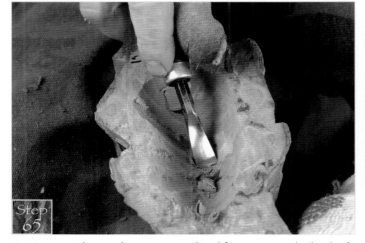

A 16 mm #5 bent palm gouge is utilized for removing the back of the carving along the centerline. It is very easy to make a mistake at this time, so proceed cautiously.

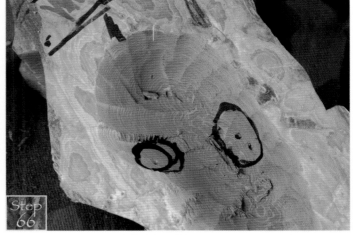

In Step 55, holes were drilled for all the windows to provide a guide to follow when hollowing out the backside of the carving. Circles have been drawn around the first two window location holes that were uncovered. Continue gouging out the back of the carving with care.

CHAPTER 3

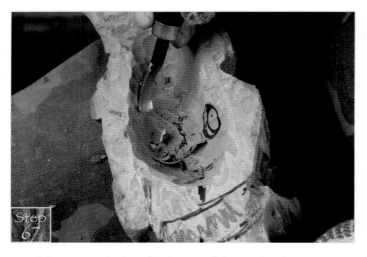

Carefully continue looking for the rest of the window location holes. It is advisable to take small, light cuts during this process.

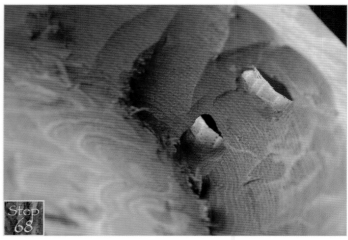

In this photo, note the ideal wall thickness of approximately ¼". As the back of the carving is being hollowed out, be sure to progress slowly, frequently stopping to note where you are in the process.

Cleaning up the tall window on the front side of the carving is made easy with the use of a stump cutter and the NSK Micromotor tool now that the back has been partially hollowed out. A knife may also be utilized for this clean-up step.

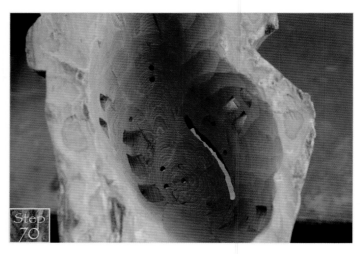

Viewing the carving from the backside, you will note the progress that has been made up to this point. Also, notice the location holes for the rest of the windows.

The NSK is utilized, along with a typhoon ball-shaped cutter, to continue hollowing out the back of the carving. If handtools are being used, various gouges could be used to smooth and clean out the back of the carving.

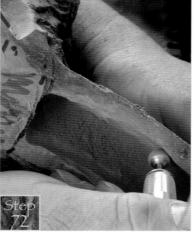

Begin hollowing out the back bottom section of the carving, maintaining at least a ½" of wall thickness at this time. This extra thickness will be utilized for carving rocks on the bottom front of the carving in a later step. Some of these rocks will be removed to allow light to show through, creating a unique look to the front of the carving. Also note that a dust collector is being used.

Looking through the window from the front side, while carving out the back, makes it easier to achieve a ¼" wall thickness.

Maintaining a ¼" wall thickness allows the use of a knife to clean the insides of the windows. When using a knife, very light, gentle cuts must be used or the cross-grained areas of the windows may break out. Don't be too concerned if the windows still contain some burn marks because these will be cleaned up at a later time.

Using a marker or a pencil, mark the area in the chimney that will be removed to form an opening for the chimney flue.

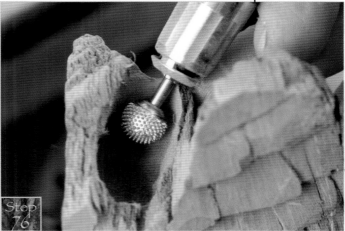

A typhoon ball cutter is being used to create an elongated hole in the chimney. A gouge could also be used to carve in the chimney hole.

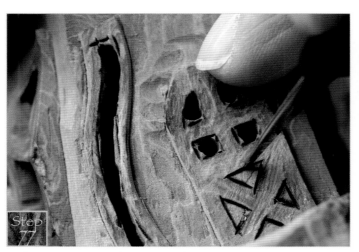

In this photo, the tip of a detail knife is being utilized to create a stop cut along the burn lines in the door panels. These panels will be set in to a depth of approximately ⅟₁₆".

The panels are being recessed on the crossbuck-style door in this photo. Due to their small size, these panels can be difficult to carve clean. Texturing will be completed in a later step to resolve this problem. Make sure to remove all burn lines that were used for the stop cuts on the door panels.

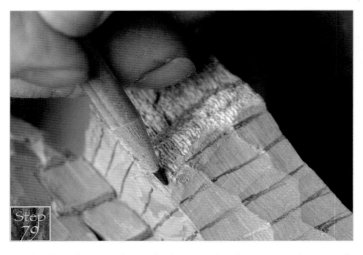

The brickwork is now being laid out on the chimney. With a pencil, begin drawing in the lines that will eventually become rows of brick.

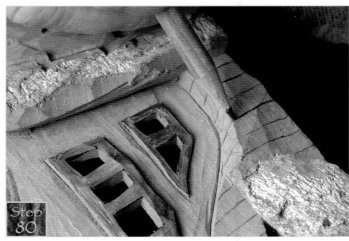

Brickwork is being added to the right side of the carving in this photo. Draw guidelines for the brick all the way to the eave of the roof. Notice how the rows of brick taper off where they begin to meet the rough bark.

Using a 4 mm v-tool, begin carving in the lines that will become rows of brick.

Begin cutting in the bricks on the right side of the carving. Notice the unevenness of the rows and the varying thickness of the bricks.

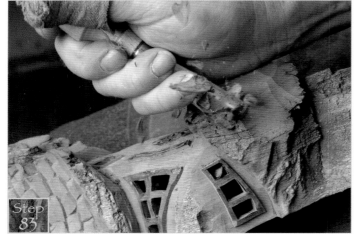

In Step 1, reference was made to the part of the bark that curved toward the left side of the carving that would become steps and rock. This photo shows a #5 gouge being used to clean off and develop this area of the carving.

Begin laying out the steps by drawing individual steps from the left side of the house to the landing by the front door.

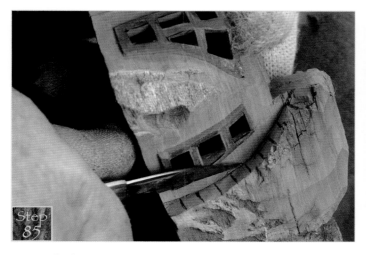

Using a knife, make a stop cut between the wall and the steps. This cut may have to be repeated a few times as each individual step is cut out.

A knife is being used to create a stop cut for each individual step. Make sure the cut is straight down.

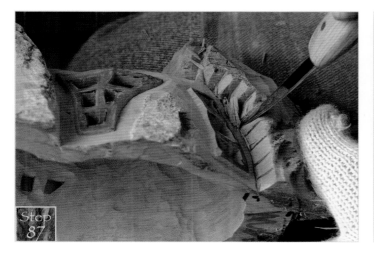

Starting at the landing by the front door, begin cutting in the steps.

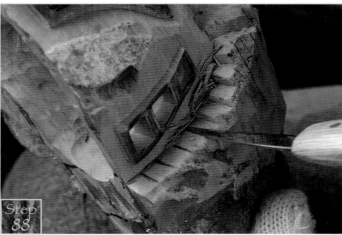

Because the cuts are being made into the end grain of the bark, make sure your knife is extremely sharp and that small cuts are taken. This will eliminate some of the tear-out experienced with cutting the end grain. Continue on, finishing the remaining steps.

The look of flagstone is being created in this section of the carving. Using a pencil or marker, draw some guidelines in for the flagstone. As always, keep some unevenness to the lines.

A large v-tool is being used in this photo to separate the individual rows of stone. Notice how the rows of stone are incorporated into the steps for a smooth transition in this area.

A knife is being used to open up and deepen some of the areas between the rows of stone. In this step, depth and unevenness will be created in the stonework, which will create a more natural look to the stone.

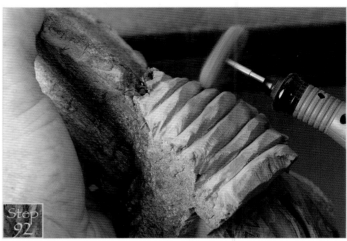

A small rotary tool is being utilized with a Scotch Brite 7440 pad to clean off all of the pencil marks made earlier. This scuffing action will soften the hard edges on the rows of stone, adding to a more natural appearance.

Using a knife, begin separating the rows of stone into individual stones.

Continue carving and separating the stones. Note how the separations are staggered and not in line like brickwork.

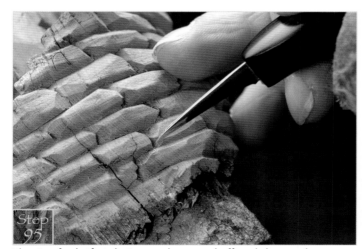

The tip of a knife is being used to round off and deepen the corners of the stonework. This will create more dimension and shadow to the stones. In a later step, power will be used to further clean up and undercut this area.

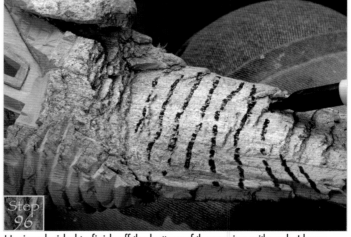

Having decided to finish off the bottom of the carving with rock, I have begun by drawing guidelines directly on the rough bark. Notice how the flagstone tapers off into the rough gray area of the bark. You will also note the natural split area that was saved in an earlier step. These two areas combined provide a unique transition to the rocks below.

Using a 12 mm v-tool, begin roughing in the rows for the rocks. Notice that the rough area of bark was not removed before cutting in the rocks. This will create a coarser texture on some of the rocks.

A knife is being utilized in this photo to open up and deepen some of the areas between the rocks. This will ensure that all of the rocks are of varying widths.

A v-tool is being used to separate the rows of rock into individual rocks. Some of the separation cuts are cut in at a slight angle, which allows for a more pleasing look to the stonework.

Using a knife, continue to shape and separate the rocks. Also, note how the rocks taper off into the natural bark area that was left on the bottom of the carving.

An NSK Micromotor tool with a coarse flame-shaped ruby bur is being utilized in this step to add some shape to the rocks. You will also notice some of the rough bark texture that will be left on the rocks. If using handtools, a knife would be used for this step.

The NSK with a needle point diamond bur is used to create a slight undercut between the rocks. This bur is also used to deepen and shape the corners of the rock, which will add further dimension and shadow.

With the back bottom section of the carving hollowed out, the needle point diamond bur is being used to open up some spaces between the rocks on the front side of the carving. This step will allow light to show through, creating a more unique appearance. A knife could also be used for this step.

Continue to open up areas between the rocks utilizing the needle point diamond bur. Additional material may have to be removed from the back of the carving in order to get the rockwork thin enough to pierce through from the front side. Continue to clean up and add in detail.

Returning to the flagstone area of the carving, begin cleaning and undercutting the stones with the needle point diamond bur.

In Steps 33-35, CA glue was used to fill in cracks and splits in the bark. The glue has left some residue on the carving that needs to be cleaned up.

With a brass brush in the NSK, use a light touch to begin cleaning and blending in the glued-up areas. This will remove most of the excess glue. Note: Safety glasses should be worn in this step.

A close-up of the roof area before cleanup is shown in this photo. A knife, along with a #3 gouge, is used for clean-up work.

Note that some of the hard edges have been softened by scuffing them with a Scotch Brite pad in a rotary tool. Some additional clean-up work will also be required.

A small butane torch is being utilized to create a burned and charred look to the chimney. Immediately after burning, use a stiff bristled brush to remove any glowing embers. (Use extreme caution when burning the chimney to avoid starting a fire. It is recommended that this burning process be completed outdoors.)

Using a triangular-shaped needle file, begin to clean up the framework around the windows. This will smooth out any rough, ragged edges that remain in the window frames.

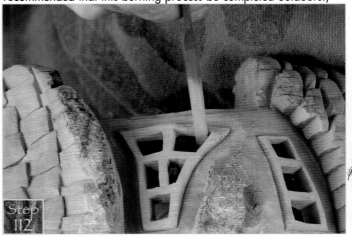

Continue cleaning the windows with the flat needle file, as shown in this photo. Note how the file fits right into the corner of the window, allowing easy cleanup of the corners. Make sure to remove all burn marks from the previously made stop cuts.

Draw in some lines to create a layered patio-stone look to the front landing. Remember to tie this in with the flagstone below.

Using a small v-tool, cut in the lines for the stonework that were laid out in the previous step.

CHAPTER 3

As referenced in Step 78, work will now begin on texturing the recessed door panels. Using a homemade tool that resembles an ice pick, push the point into the panel repeatedly, creating a rough background.

Using a knife, make a light stop cut on the inside of the window frame. The stop cut should be approximately 1/16" deep.

A long bent #3 gouge is being used to remove a small slice of bark to the stop cut made in the previous step. Notice how the completed cut starts in the center of the vertical mullion and continues to the outer framework.

In this photo, another view is shown of the inner frame being set in from the outer framework. Use extreme caution when making these cuts because the bark can break quite easily. Note that no cuts have been made in the center part of the window. These cuts are not set in because the center is easily broken.

Continue setting in all the window frames on the remainder of the carving. By setting in the window frames, a slight reveal between the inner and outer framework has been achieved, which will create a nice shadow line when the work is completed.

To create vertical siding or boards, begin by drawing them in with a marker, avoiding drawing straight lines.

Step 121

A small v-tool is being used to cut in the lines for the siding. Note that straight lines in the siding have been avoided, adding to the whimsical look of the creation.

Step 122

After all vertical lines have been cut in, horizontal splices are added to the siding. Randomly draw in the splice lines, avoiding any set pattern and continuing to avoid straight lines.

Step 123

A small v-tool is being used to cut in the splice lines on the siding in this photo.

Step 124

A double ball end stylus is being utilized to create the look of nail holes. Lightly push the stylus into the bark, creating a slight indent.

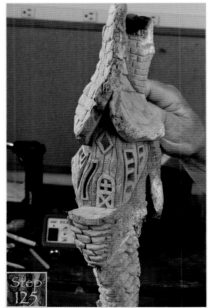

Step 125

The completed carving is shown in this photo. One last cleanup will take place at this point, and then the scuffing process will begin. The complete carving is scuffed using a Scotch Brite 7440 pad and a rotary tool. Scuffing allows softening of any hard lines that were created in the carving process. Remember to use a light touch when scuffing since the Scotch Brite 7440 pad is quite abrasive.

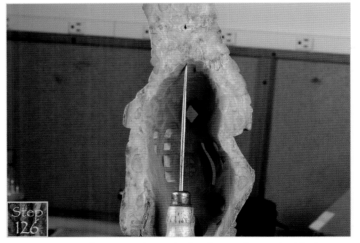

Step 126

Using an ice pick or something similar, locate the vertical balance point on the back of the carving, and mark it for drilling.

CHAPTER 3

A small hand drill with a ¼" drill bit is being utilized in this step to drill a hole in the back of the carving for hanging. Note that the hole is drilled at a slightly upward angle.

The last step before applying the finish is to sign the carving. A woodburner with a writing tip is being used to sign the carving in an out-of-the-way place on the front side.

Before applying the finish to the carving, be sure to read the section on finishing in this book. Having removed all dust from the carving, begin spraying Deft on the backside of the carving, as shown in this photo. Note that this process is being completed outdoors.

Spray the front side of the carving while holding it at an angle, allowing the spray to reach under the roof.

After the first coat of Deft is dry, rub down the entire carving with a piece of crumpled brown paper bag. The crumpled bag acts as a super-fine sandpaper, removing any roughness and smoothing the entire surface of the carving prior to adding additional coats of Deft. Be sure to use the crumpled brown bag between each coat of finish and to remove all dust before applying additional coats. Use as many coats as needed on the front and backsides to build up an even sheen. If the finish becomes too shiny, spray it with a light coat of Krylon Matte Finish to reduce the shine.

Begin applying a 50/50 mix of Watco Wax with a brush, starting with the backside of the carving and continuing on to the front. After the wax has been applied, wipe the carving off with a cotton rag to remove excess wax. Using the rag, wipe out the brush so that it's dry before proceeding to brush out the pooled areas of wax on the surface of the carving. Set the carving aside to dry for a minimum of 24 hours before completing the final buffing process. Buff the carving carefully to a soft luster with a horsehair shoe brush or a rotary brush. The step-by-step process is now complete.

This photo shows the right side of the finished carving.

The left side of the finished carving is pictured in this photo.

REVIEW

The following photos show many views of the finished house carving. It is my hope that these in-depth looks at the piece after it has been completed will help you to better understand the carving process.

This photo illustrates the natural, rough bark shape that was left on the carving, adding to its uniqueness and charm. Traces of the CA Glue, which was utilized in this area, are no longer visible.

Be sure to make use of natural shapes in the bark. Note how the bricks mysteriously disappear into the dark recesses of the split.

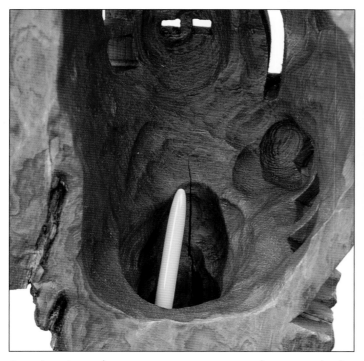

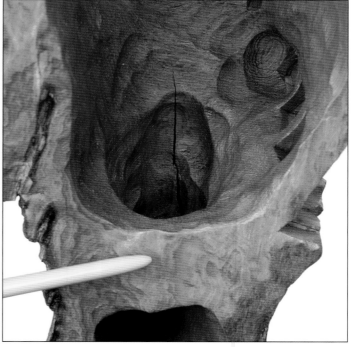

Sometimes it may become necessary to open up the area under the bridge to gain access to the windows.

This photo illustrates the bridge area, which was left to hold the carving together to keep it from collapsing.

The tiny woodland spirits that live here have been using this chimney for years. Burning out the chimney has added a myth-like quality to the work.

This photo shows the hollowed-out and curved appearance of the roof, which has created additional charisma in this whimsical creation.

The rough bark area provides a natural transition from the flagstone on the front door landing to the brickwork on the side of the house. Be sure to take advantage of these rough bark areas.

The wax that was applied to the carving during the finishing stages has darkened the area between and under the stonework, creating even greater definition.

Notice the depth of the roof overhang. Creating areas like this greatly enhances the overall appearance of the finished carving.

Note how the rough gray bark area adds appeal to the bulged-out wall section of the house. Following completion of the finishing process, the nail holes and texture on the doors really stand out.

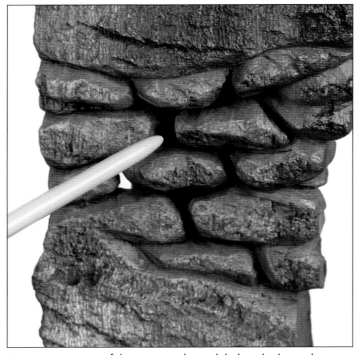

Opening up some of the areas in the rock below the house has created an added element of whimsy. Will the rocks hold together over time, or will the tiny woodland spirits have to repair them?

Be proud of your work, and sign it with your name or logo on an out-of-the-way spot on the front side of the carving. You may also want to date your piece. I rarely date my carvings, unless they are commissions or are being given as gifts.

Carving Tree Bark in the Round

 Many people consider the ideal piece of bark for carving to be at least five inches thick, five to six inches wide and 18 to 24 inches long. That's true—if you are carving a whimsical house. However, there is a great way to use those smaller pieces of bark that are often labeled unusable: Try carving them in the round.

I enjoy carving bark in this manner because it allows me to be creative with the "throw-away" pieces of bark that have split during harvesting or are left over from my larger projects. In my classes, I consider this in-the-round bark tree a great practice piece for carving in-the-round bark Santas.

The piece of cottonwood bark I am using here is about six to eight inches long. It is $1^{1}/_{2}$" an in diameter at the base. To carve this piece, you will need a detail knife, a longer bladed knife and a 6 mm #11 gouge. As with any bark carving project, your tools must be very sharp.

Carving bark in the round gives the bark carver a great look at the properties of bark. Because square trees don't exist, this project allows you to see how the bark reacts when you are carving all the way around the bark. You'll note that chipping and flaking are two common occurrences. These potentially damaging happenings can be somewhat controlled by using the special cuts mentioned in Chapter 2.

I always try to leave some rough bark somewhere on the finished carving. This touch adds uniqueness to the finished piece and gives the viewer a hint about what kind of wood the piece was created from. I also paint the piece with light washes to allow some of the rough areas and the golden reddish tones show through.

> It is recommended that the complete step-by-step process be reviewed before beginning this project.

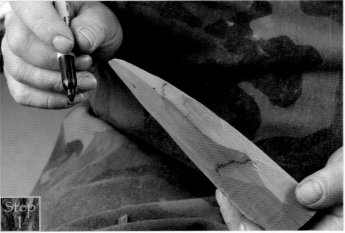

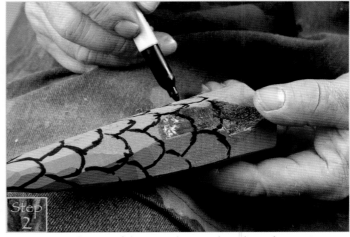

With a bandsaw, begin by shaping a piece of cottonwood bark into the shape of a tree. Using the saw, trim the edges off, giving the blank a somewhat rounded shape. The edges of the blank could also be removed with a knife. The photo illustrates the tree blank being laid out with the use of a marker.

Beginning at the top of the tree, draw in three branch sections resembling elongated fish scales. All of the remaining branches will radiate out from these three sections. Notice how the branch sections become larger, both in length and width, as they are laid out to the bottom of the tree.

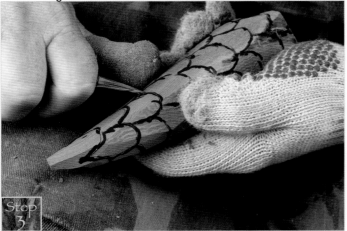

Begin carving by cutting in stop cuts with the tip of a knife to the approximate depth of ⅛" along the lines drawn in the previous step. These stop cuts will be cut in deeper as the carving progresses and starts to take shape.

Continue with the second row of branches, carving up to the stop cut made in the previous step.

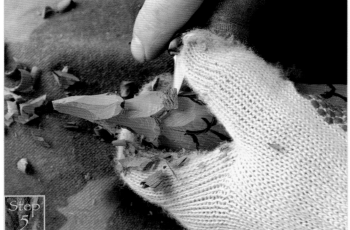

Notice how the second row of branches tucks under the top row and how the third row of branches goes under the second row. This pattern will continue for the remainder of the tree. A knife is used to create a slight curl. Notice how the individual branches have been separated, just like the shingles on the house carving.

Using a 4 mm or 6 mm #11 gouge, begin texturing the individual branches. Create soft curves when adding this texture, avoiding straight lines. A v-tool could also be used when adding texture.

Note the texturing and the depth of the branches as shown in this photo.

After the texturing is complete, clean and soften the tree, utilizing a light scuffing technique with a Scotch Brite pad. This scuffing will soften all of the hard lines created by the tools during the carving process.

Create a mixture of pine green and Pthalo green acrylic paint with lots of water added to form a thin wash. Apply this mixture to the tree with a large brush. The thin paint allows the golden brown tones of the bark to show through.

This photo shows the first wash of paint completed. Dry this wash of paint with a hairdryer, and then proceed to apply two additional washes of the paint mixture, drying after each coat.

Using a ¾" wide, flat paintbrush, dry brush some ivory paint onto the carving using a very light touch. To dry brush, load the paintbrush with paint and wipe most of it off on a paper towel. Lightly drag the brush across the branches so that the high areas pick up some of the ivory paint. You will note that some of the brown tones of the bark will still be visible. After the painting is completed, the same finishing techniques will be utilized as were used for the completion of the whimsical bark house.

Chapter Five

Finishing Bark Carvings

 am often asked how I achieve such a unique, soft, touchable finish on my works. The secret is in the combination of lacquers and waxes.

LACQUER AND WAX FINISH

My preferred finish is a combination of lacquer and wax. The lacquer I recommend is an aerosol semi-gloss made by Deft. It is important to remember that any time a lacquer or varnish is used it will darken the wood. When waxing, I use Watco Satin Finishing Wax.

STEP ONE: DUST REMOVAL

The first step in the finishing process is to remove all of the dust from your carving. Dust removal can be accomplished by using compressed air, a brush or a vacuum.

STEP TWO: LACQUER

The next step in the process would be to evenly spray Deft on the back of the piece, making sure to get complete coverage in the hollowed out areas and avoiding runs. After a few minutes of drying time, turn the piece over and spray the front, following the same procedure. Try to avoid spraying finish on the natural roughness, or gray area, of the bark.

Upon allowing the entire first coat to dry, use a piece of thoroughly crumpled brown paper bag to rub the entire carving. This removes all fuzzy and high spots that the lacquer created since the bag acts as an ultra-fine sandpaper, preparing the surface for the next coat of finish. Remove any remaining dust, and repeat the lacquering process again.

Applying a third coat of Deft will seal the carving and build a depth to the finish, resulting in a slight gloss and an even sheen all over the carving. Additional coats may be added as desired.

I prefer a satin, rather than a shiny, finish to my pieces, so I choose not to use a high-gloss finish. If a carving is too shiny for my liking, I will sometimes spray on a coat of Krylon matte finish to dull the sheen. If using Krylon, spray a light mist about 15 inches away from the piece.

Note: Lacquer does not dry clear when applied in a highly humid area. If humidity is unavoidable, spray your carving outdoors, and move it into an air-conditioned area to dry.

Woodland Hide-A-Way
2¼" thick, 3¾" wide,
8" long
Carved from Eastern
Cottonwood Bark;
shoe cream finish

STEP THREE: WAX

Following lacquering, the next step in finishing is waxing. I prefer to use a 50/50 mixture of Watco Neutral Satin Finishing Wax and Watco Dark Satin Finishing Wax. Begin by using a china bristle brush to apply the mixed wax to the carving. Brush the wax on the back of the carving and then the front. Again, try to avoid the roughness of the bark, or the gray-colored areas.

After applying the wax, use a soft cotton cloth to wipe the entire carving, removing excess wax. Once this step is complete, use the dried brush to brush out the areas where the wax has pooled or is rather thick.

Set the piece aside for the wax to dry completely. This takes a minimum of two hours, but the carving can be left for as long as needed, up to months. Once the wax has dried, buff it with a shoe brush or with a rotary horsehair brush on a flex shaft machine or drill. This completes the lacquer and wax finishing process.

CLEAR WAX FINISH

I sometimes use a clear wax finish, rather than the Deft and Watco Wax combination, because of the color of the bark. Some pieces of bark will have a unique, hard-to-find color, often referred to as Montana gold. When I want to preserve this color and show it off, I use Briwax because it does not color the wood as it dries.

In this process, begin by removing the dust from your carving before applying the wax with a stencil brush or old, soft tooth-brush. Make certain the wax is completely worked into the wood, leaving no excess. Again, do not apply wax to the natural roughness, or gray-colored areas, of the bark.

As with the Watco Wax, buff the dry carving using an old shoe brush or a soft cotton cloth. A flex shaft machine or a drill with a rotary brush provides a power option. It may take two to five coats of wax to build up the desired sheen.

SHOE POLISH

Yet another type of finish I choose to use is ordinary shoe polish or shoe cream. Begin by dusting the piece. Use a stencil brush to apply a neutral cream to the front and back of the carving. Once the cream is dry, buff it off and apply a second coat of neutral cream to both sides. Additional coats may be required to obtain the desired sheen, buffing off each coat after it has dried. Drying time is dependent on the humidity in your area. The more humidity, the longer the polish will take to dry.

The drawback to this type of finish is its unknown preservation qualities. I am aware of a piece that was finished in shoe creams twenty-five years ago and still appears fine.

Another use for shoe polish or cream is to apply colored polish in certain areas after the initial finish is laid down, if preferred. Typically, I don't use color unless I have a tree or something else I wish to accent on a carving I am finishing. I might choose to add some color to the rocks or the shingles on the rooftops of my whimsical bark houses to add shadow and definition.

When finishing a piece, it is very important to read and follow all directions and safety precautions on finishing products before and during use.

Applying a Shoe Cream Finish

Step 1

Step 2

Montana Gold bark was utilized for the carving illustrated in this photo. In an attempt to retain as much of the gold color as possible, a shoe cream will be utilized for the finish. Using Meltonian Boot and Shoe Cream in a neutral shade, begin applying it to the carving with a china bristle brush. A stencil brush or soft toothbrush will provide the same results. Work the shoe cream thoroughly into the surface of the carving, avoiding any areas of polish buildup. I prefer the use of shoe cream, rather than shoe polish, because it is a soft and smooth finish medium that is quite easy to work with.

After the first coat of shoe polish is dry, buff it with a horsehair shoe brush, similar to the process utilized in buffing shoes. After buffing, apply a second coat of polish, again working it thoroughly into the surface of the carving. Set the carving aside to dry.

Step 3

Completed carving with shoe cream finish retained the gold color. Read the chapter on finishes before proceeding.

Step 4

With a rotary horsehair brush mounted in a Foredom flex shaft machine, the second coat of polish is buffed out to a soft sheen.

Using Paint

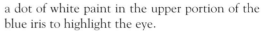

o begin the painting process, I make certain that my carving is very clean, containing no dark marks or smudges. I often use Scotch Brite 7440 pads on a rotary tool to clean up my bark carvings. This not only cleans pencil lines and smudges from the carving, but it also softens the hard edges that are leftover from the carving process. After scuffing, I make sure that I remove all the dust and dirt; then paint acrylic washes directly on the wood.

To begin painting a Santa such as the one pictured here, I find it best to start with the face. I use a thinned-down flesh tone, painting over the face, including the eyes and the eyebrows. While the paint is still wet, I blend a darker flesh tone or red iron oxide into the lower cheek area. I also like to blend in a bit of the darker tone on the tip of the nose.

The next step in painting is the mouth. I use the same flesh tone as on the face, blending in the darker flesh color on the lips. If the mouth is open, I will add a little red onto the tongue. I do not overdo the red because a little goes a long way.

I then paint the hair and the beard areas and move on to the fur trim. For the hair and the fur, I prefer to use an off-white or a shade of ivory, rather than a pure white. I thin the paint down so it is nearly translucent and apply it to the areas I wish to cover. To check for missed spots, I usually use a bright light or take my piece outdoors and look it over carefully, making sure that I didn't miss any spots in the beard or in the trim areas on the carving.

Next, I paint the eyes. Using thick ivory paint, I paint the entire eyeball. When that has dried, I paint the iris of the eye in my chosen color. When painting the iris, I will mix the chosen color with flow medium on a one-to-one ratio. Flow medium mixed with acrylic paints will thin the paint and allow for easier brushing, while retaining the full color of the paint.

My carvings never have eyes that look straight ahead. (My reasoning behind this is that if one eye is a bit out of alignment, the carving gives off a frightening look.) For example, using blue as the eye color, I position the iris in the corner of the eye, focusing on the direction I want my Santa to be looking. In order to paint the iris, I use straight blue paint with flow medium added. When the blue is dry, I paint the black pupil, leaving a small amount of the blue showing. When the black paint is dry, I place a dot of white paint in the upper portion of the blue iris to highlight the eye.

Moving on to the next painting step, I use a mixture of burnt sienna and a lot of water to form a translucent color that works great for mittens, boots, belts, toy bags and the leather strap on the sleigh bells. For the bells themselves, I use either gold or silver metallic paint mixed with one part paint to one part flow medium.

The final color in Santa painting is, of course, red. There are many, many different reds available. I choose a favorite and usually add some burnt umber to tone the red down slightly. Once the red is mixed, I add water, and then some more water, and probably a bit more water after that. I always test my paint on a piece of scrap wood to see if I have achieved the correct color and paint thickness. I should be able to see the wood grain showing through the paint. If after the first coat, I prefer a deeper color, I apply a second wash. The most important thing I remember to do is to thin my paint. When teaching seminars, I am accused of going home with more paint than I bring, which is basically the truth.

Now that the carving is painted, it is time for sealing. My first step is to make sure the paint is completely dry, not even slightly damp. My personal preference is to use Deft semi-gloss spray to seal my carvings. I apply a medium coat and let it dry. Then, I rub the carving down with a piece of crumpled-up brown paper bag. Next, I clean it off with a tack cloth to remove the dust and then spray it again with Deft. I continue this process until I have built up an even sheen on the entire carving, paying particular attention to the end grain. When the carving has a consistent gloss, I again rub it with a piece of brown paper bag. For the final coat of sealer, I use Krylon matte finish #1311 to dull the shine.

Now comes the fun part! For antiquing, I use Watco Satin Finishing Wax in dark and neutral. I use a large brush to apply a 50/50 mix and immediately wipe the carving down with a lint-free cloth. I brush out some of the facial features with a dry brush, often wiping the brush on the lint-free cloth, pulling off as much of the antiquing as I desire. Finally, I allow the carving to dry overnight and then buff it with a shoe brush the next day. The result is a very lovely, soft, satin-type finish.

PAINTING RED

There are many, many shades of red. The following are my favorite reds for holiday bark carvings of Santa Claus.

DELTA CERAMCOAT

TOMATO SPICE

Use for garments. This is my top paint choice for bark because it keeps its nice red tone when it is made into a wash. Most of the Santas in this book were painted with Tomato Spice.

RED IRON OXIDE

Use on face for blush, nose, cheeks and lips. This is not a powerful red like tomato spice. It is a rust-colored red that would work well for a frontiersman Santa or woodsman Santa.

MENDOCINO RED

Use for old world Santas. This burgandy red is beautiful on bark.

NORSK BLUE

It's not red, but it is the next best color for Santas carved in the Scandinavian style.

AMERICANA

COUNTRY RED

Use for new age or modern Santas. This is a bright, vibrant red.

SANTA RED

If you're looking for a brighter-than-bright red, this is your red. Santa red is the brightest red on this list.

FOLK ART

CHRISTMAS RED

Use for holly berries. This is a bright, bold color, but a little duller than Country or Santa Red.

JO SONJA'S

BURGUNDY

Use on old world Santas. This paint gives a nice, dark, red tone. Three or four light washes will still allow you to see the wood underneath.

PERMANENT ALIZARINE

This lighter shade of burgundy looks great on old world Santas.

METALLICS

Again, they aren't red, but Jo Sonja's gold colors are great for gold beading and buckles.

Chapter Six

Patterns

WOOD SPIRIT INSPIRATIONS

atterns aren't typically used when creating wood spirits out of cottonwood bark although I sometimes use drawings to assist with achieving the outcome that I desire. For sources of inspiration, I've included some examples of wood spirits using black and white line drawings only, which I feel more clearly illustrate the depth and shadow of the piece without the added distraction of color. The drawings illustrated on the follow pages were created from existing bark carvings in my collection.

It's a good idea to sketch out your ideas before you begin to carve a spirit face. Design the face to fit the uniqueness of the piece of bark, taking advantage of the natural shapes and splits in the bark when laying out your wood spirit. Sometimes I will trace the outline of the piece of bark on a large piece of paper and sketch in the features I'm planning to carve to provide an idea of the final layout of the piece. I do basically the same thing with the side profile of the piece to illustrate the depth that I am planning to achieve. Make use of this depth to ensure that the face doesn't become too flat. These two steps will eliminate a lot of frustration before you begin the actual carving and will help in creating a piece that flows from one area to the other.

It is my hope that these drawings will provide some inspiration as you create your spirit faces out of cottonwood bark. Remember, you don't have to play by the rules that govern realistic faces, as these are whimsical wood spirits that are limited only by your own imagination.

Legend of the Wood Spirit
as told by Rick Jensen

Etched in the history of the Old Country is the legend of the wood spirit, which is based on ancient shepherd tales from a time when all the land was owned by kings and noblemen.

Shepherd peasants had few possessions and were not permitted to own land. For firewood, they were allowed only to pick up fallen, dead wood on the ground. Soon their sources became scarce.

They petitioned the king to issue a decree allowing them to pull the dead branches, within their reach, from the trees. The wise peasants soon learned to use their shepherd's crooks, which were formed with a hook on the end, to reach higher into the trees in order to pull down more branches. Thus came about the saying, "By hook or by crook."

The shepherd peasants, being somewhat superstitious, believed that a spirit dwelled deep within each tree. By carving a face into the pieces of wood, the spirit would be released and good luck would be bestowed upon them.

Sources for Cottonwood Bark

THE BARK GUY
Art Olver
568 Valentine Ave. S.E.
Pacific, WA 98047
Telephone: 253-804-3488
E-Mail: artolver@comcast.net

CHIPPING AWAY, INC.
808 Courtland Ave. East
Kitchener, ON N2C 1K3 Canada
Telephone: 1-888-682-9801
Website: www.woodcarvingstore.com
(Our bark is from Northern British
Columbia and is therefore extra thick
and wide. Averages 3" to 5" thick,
width varies. Sold in ½ lb.
increments. Extra long pieces
available by special request.)

RICK JENSEN
720 Pine St.
Crookston, MN 56716
E-Mail: jrjensen@gvtel.com
(I also teach a number of bark carving
seminars at various locations
throughout the year.
For seminar information, contact me
at the above address.)

More Great Project Books from Fox Chapel Publishing

Wood Spirits and Green Men
A Design Sourcebook for Woodcarvers and Other Artists
By Lora S. Irish, Chris Pye, Shawn Cipa
Pages 104
ISBN: 1-56523-261-5
$19.95

Carving Found Wood
Tips Techniques & Inspiration from the Artists
by: Vic Hood, Jack A. Williams
Pages: 96
ISBN: 1-56523-159-7
$19.95

Extreme Pumpkin Carving
20 Amazing designs from Frightful to Fabulous
By Vic Hood, Jack A. Williams
Pages 96
ISBN: 1-56523-213-5
$14.95

Caricature Carving from Head to Toe
A Complete Step-by-Step Guide to Capturing Expression and Humor in Wood
By Dave Stetson
Pages 96
ISBN: 1-56523-121-X
$19.95

Art of Stylized Wood Carving
By David Hamilton, Charles Solomon
Pages 112
ISBN: 1-56523-174-0
$19.95

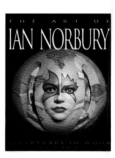

Art of Ian Norbury
Sculptures in Wood
By Ian Norbury
Pages 160
ISBN: 1-56523-222-4
$24.95

LOOK FOR THESE BOOKS AT YOUR LOCAL BOOK STORE OR WOODWORKING RETAILER
Or call 800-457-9112 • Visit www.FoxChapelPublishing.com

Learn from the Experts

Fox Chapel Publishing is not only your leading resource for woodworking books, but also the publisher of the two leading how-to magazines for woodcarvers and woodcrafters!

WOOD CARVING ILLUSTRATED is the leading how-to magazine for woodcarvers of all skill levels and styles—providing inspiration and instruction from some of the world's leading carvers and teachers. A wide range of step-by-step projects are presented in an easy-to-follow format, with great photography and useful tips and techniques. *Wood Carving Illustrated* delivers quality editorial on the most popular carving styles, such as realistic and stylized wildlife carving, power carving, Santas, caricatures, chip carving and fine art carving. The magazine also includes tool reviews, painting and finishing features, profiles on carvers, photo galleries and more.

SCROLL SAW WORKSHOP is the leading how-to magazine for novice and professional woodcrafters. Shop-tested projects are complete with patterns and detailed instructions. The casual scroller appreciates the in-depth information that ensures success and yields results that are both useful and attractive; the pro will be creatively inspired with fresh and innovative design ideas. Each issue of *Scroll Saw Workshop* contains useful news, hints and tips, and includes lively features and departments that bring the world of scrolling to the reader.

Want to learn more about a subscription? **Visit www.FoxChapelPublishing.com** and click on either the *Wood Carving Illustrated* button or *Scroll Saw Workshop* button at the top of the page. Watch for our special **FREE ISSUE** offer! Or call toll-free at 1-800-457-9112.